Bar

Making History

By Adria F. Klein

HAMERAY
PUBLISHING GROUP

Published in the United States of America
by the Hameray Publishing Group, Inc.

Every effort has been made to trace copyright holders and obtain their
permission for use of copyright material. The publisher will gladly
receive information enabling them to rectify any error or omission in
subsequent editions. All facts are correct at time of going to press.

Text © Adria F. Klein
Published 2009

Publisher: Raymond Yuen
Series Editors: Adria F. Klein and Alan Trussell-Cullen
Project Editor: Kaitlyn Nichols
Designers: Lois Stanfield and Linda Lockowitz

Photo Credits: Getty: cover and pages 1, 4, 27
AP: back cover and pages 7, 13, 18, 26, 28, 31, 33
Corbis: pages 8, 16, 23

All rights reserved. No part of this publication may be reproduced
or transmitted in any form or by any means without permission in
writing from the publisher. Reproduction of any part of this book,
through photocopy, recording, or any electronic or mechanical
retrieval system without the written permission of the publisher,
is an infringement of the copyright law.

ISBN 978-1-60559-055-4

Printed in the U.S.A.

1 2 3 4 5 LP 13 12 11 10 09

Contents

Chapter 1

Looking Ahead

August 28, 2008 was a very important night. The Democratic Party was holding their **convention** to **nominate**, or pick, a person to run for president. A quiet Barack Obama stood backstage in Denver where the convention was being held. He heard his name announced. He heard the roar from the crowd.

It was a historic moment. Barack Obama was the first African-American candidate selected from a major party to run for president of the United States. In just over

◄ Senator Obama gives a speech during the Democratic National Convention.

two months, the national **election** for president would be held. Two short months and so much to do.

Barack Obama walked out to the front of the stage to give his speech. The crowd went wild. He put his large hands up to quiet the cheers. The **senator** from the state of Illinois was ready for the challenge of leading the nation.

> *"We cannot walk alone. At this moment, in this election, we must pledge to march into the future. Let us keep that promise, that American promise."*
>
> —Barack Obama

Chapter 2

Family Roots

Barack Obama was born on August 4, 1961, in Honolulu, Hawaii. His father, Barack Obama Sr., was from Kenya, a country in east Africa. He was a member of the Luo tribe. His mother, Stanley Ann Dunham, called Ann, grew up in Kansas.

► Barack's mother Ann raised Barack as a single parent.

▲ Barack playing baseball as a child growing up in Hawaii.

She moved to Hawaii with her family after World War II.

Barack's father and mother met at the University of Hawaii. His father came to Hawaii on a **scholarship**. They were both students at the university and while they were very young, they fell in love.

They faced many challenges going to school and raising a child. Under all this pressure, Barack's parents separated when he was two years old. His father returned to Kenya after studying for his **doctorate** at Harvard University. Barack would only see his father one more time when Barack was ten years old.

Barack's mother went back to school and met Lolo Soetoro at the university. She soon married him. Soetoro was from Indonesia and when Barack was six, the family moved there.

Barack went to school in Indonesia and learned the Indonesian language. In school he went by his nickname, Barry. His mother taught him lessons in English. She woke him up early every morning to study before he went to school.

While they were in Indonesia, his parents had another baby, his half sister Maya. Her name is now Maya Soetoro-Ng.

Chapter 3

Growing Up

When Barack was ten, his mother separated from Lolo Soetoro. His mother's parents were living in Hawaii. She wanted Barack to study in English so she sent him back to Hawaii to live with his grandparents. Barack's mother and sister soon joined him there.

Barack called his grandfather "Gramps" and his grandmother "Toot." Toot is short for "tutu," which means grandmother in Hawaiian. They helped his mother look after Barack and his sister while their mother worked and went back to school.

The school Barack went to was Punahou Academy. It was here that he became aware of

racism. He learned that having a black father and a white mother meant he was of a mixed racial background. He was teased for being different because of his skin color. Barack felt he didn't fit in at school. He looked for ways to let out his angry feelings about being teased.

His grandfather and friends encouraged him to play basketball. It was a sport he was good at and enjoyed. The basketball court was a place where he felt he fit in. Barack also understood what it meant to study hard and he graduated with honors in 1979.

> *"There's not a black America and white America and Latino America and Asian America; there's the United States of America."* —Barack Obama

▲ Barack and his teammates on the Punahou High
School basketball team in 1977. He still loves to play
basketball today!

Chapter 4

College Years and Beyond

Obama went on to study at Occidental College in Los Angeles for two years and then at Columbia University in New York. During his time in New York, he felt he learned a lot more about racism and **prejudice** in America. He experienced prejudice on the streets of New York and from some of the students at Columbia. This made him want to know more about **civil rights**. He decided to learn more about how the government worked and about human rights and the law, so he chose to study **political science**.

Obama graduated from Columbia in 1983. He hoped to go to Kenya after his graduation.

He wanted to see his father and learn more about his life. But that hope was lost when his father was killed in a car crash. Barack was only twenty-one at the time.

After college, Obama worked at Business International Corporation. He did very well, but he didn't feel he was doing the work he wanted. He wanted to do more to help people, especially people who had experienced racism like he had.

Obama moved to Chicago, Illinois, where he took a job as a community organizer. He worked with the Developing Communities Project (DCP). He helped people find housing and jobs. Most of the people he helped in Chicago were black and poor.

Obama was driven to do more. He wanted to help people get treated fairly and have equal rights. He decided he needed a law degree to help him do this.

▲ Obama graduated from Harvard University Law School in 1991.

Chapter 5

Barack and Michelle Obama

In the fall of 1988, Barack Obama entered Harvard University Law School. He was a top student and received many honors. He was the first African-American to be elected as the editor of the *Harvard Law Review*. His views were **liberal** but he was willing to listen to all sides of an issue. He learned to support his beliefs by talking with different people and listening to their views.

During the summer after his first year of law school, Obama took a job back in Chicago with a law firm. There he met Michelle Robinson. She was younger than Barack but had finished law school before him. It was her

job to train him for his summer job at the law firm.

Michelle Robinson was from Chicago and of African-American heritage, or background. She attended Princeton University and also graduated from Harvard University Law School. Michelle and Barack had a lot in common. They had encountered many of the same challenges growing up. They fell in love and married three years later in 1992 at the Trinity United Church of Christ in Chicago. They began their life together working for the same causes and goals. They shared the same beliefs and commitments and still do. It is a wonderful partnership.

◀ Barack and Michelle met at a law firm in Chicago and were married in 1992.

Chapter 6

Barack Obama Becomes a Senator

Barack and Michelle both worked in Chicago as lawyers. Obama also continued to work in the community. He helped organize voter registration drives in Chicago when Bill Clinton ran for president.

Obama had been working on his first book about his life for several years. *Dreams from My Father* was published in 1995. In it, he talked about the challenges he faced in his upbringing, the stories he heard, and the lessons he learned.

In 1995, just after his book was published, Barack Obama's mother passed away. She had been living in Hawaii and he had stayed close to her. Now both his mother and father were gone, along with his grandfather. The loss of those close to him deepened his understanding of the importance of family.

Obama wanted to find a way to help more people and decided to run for Illinois state senator. He ran as a Democrat in his first election in 1996 and won. He represented the same part of Chicago that he had worked in as a community organizer.

Obama served two terms as a state senator and helped to pass many laws to help people. He was successful because he was **open-minded**. Like his time in law school, he listened to different people and to all sides

> *"If you're walking down the right path and you're willing to keep walking, eventually you'll make progress."* —Barack Obama

of an issue. As a state senator, he worked with both Democrats and Republicans to help the people of Illinois.

Democrats and Republicans

The Democratic Party and the Republican Party are the two main political parties, or organizations, in the United States.

In 1999 Michelle and Barack Obama had their first child, a daughter named Malia. Their second daughter, Natasha, called Sasha, was born in 2001.

The attack on the United States on September 11, 2001, changed so many things for all people. Barack Obama wanted to do more and work harder to help people after the tragedy.

Michelle, Malia, Sasha, and Barack Obama in 2008. ▶

Obama was against going to war with Iraq. In 2003, just after the war began, he decided to run for the United States Senate. His powerful speeches reached the hearts of people. In November 2004 he won the election with 70% of the vote. Barack Obama was now a United States senator representing the whole state of Illinois.

> *"Today we begin in earnest the work of making sure that the world we leave our children is just a little bit better than the one we inhabit today."*
> —Barack Obama

Chapter 7

Running for the Highest Office in the Land

Obama began his work in the U.S. Senate with the same energy and strengths he had shown throughout his young life and his schooling. He served on many important committees in the Senate and helped to pass many laws. He shared his political beliefs, but continued to be open-minded and work for positive change.

He wrote a second book in 2006, *The Audacity of Hope: Thoughts on Reclaiming the American Dream.* In it, he shared his beliefs and offered his ideas for change that would reawaken the American dream.

In February 2007 Obama announced his **candidacy** for president of the United States.

▲ Barack Obama made history by becoming the first African-American presidential nominee.

Obama with his vice-presidential running mate, Senator Joe Biden from Delaware. ▶

He fought a tough but fair **campaign** for the nomination. He selected Senator Joe Biden from Delaware as his vice-presidential running mate. Together, they worked hard to talk to many people and share their beliefs.

After winning the nomination, they had two short months to take their message to the country and get voters on their side.

▲ President-elect Barack Obama celebrates his victory with his family.

Chapter 8

President Obama

November 4, 2008 was the big day. It was the day everyone voted for the president. Barack and Michelle Obama voted in Chicago. Obama took a break to play some basketball and then he did some last minute campaigning.

As the voting ended, polling places around the country closed. Everyone waited for the results. The Obamas were in Chicago with their family, friends, and people who had worked on the campaign.

Obama supporters gathered together all over the country to watch the results on television. In Chicago, more than 250,000 Obama supporters gathered in Grant Park.

They waited to hear Obama speak after the results of the election. Millions more all over the world waited for the outcome.

The news on television began to report the returns of the voting. Slowly, excitement built as each state reported its results. Barack Obama and Joe Biden were together in Chicago. They talked with each other and their families, waiting for the results. Their excitement grew as they watched the news.

"If there is anyone out there who still doubts that America is a place where all things are possible, who still wonders if the dream of our founders is alive in our time, who still questions the power of our democracy, tonight is your answer."
—Barack Obama, in his victory speech

▲ Obama supporters show their excitement at Grant Park.

It was ten o'clock in Chicago when the announcement was made. Barack Obama had made history. He was elected as the first African-American president of the United States in a landslide victory. The crowd at

Grant Park went wild. All over the country, people were celebrating. Some shouted, some sang, some cried tears of happiness. It was a historic moment for America. Once they heard the results of the election, they waited to hear Obama's victory speech.

Obama walked on to the stage in front of his cheering supporters. Obama had inspired millions of people. In his speech, he thanked all those that helped him along the way. He promised that he would work hard to bring prosperity, peace, and hope back to America. "Yes we can!" Obama said in his victory speech. "Yes we can!" America replied.

> *"I will never forget who this victory truly belongs to. It belongs to you . . . This is your victory."*
> —**Barack Obama**, in his victory speech

▲ Barack Obama made history when he won the
presidential election on November 4, 2008.

Timeline

1961 Born on August 4, in Hawaii

1967 Moved to Indonesia with his mother
and stepfather

1971 Moved to Hawaii and lived with his
grandparents

1979 Graduated from Punahou High School
with honors

1983 Graduated from Columbia University
with honors, majoring in political
science

1991 Graduated from Harvard University Law
School with honors

1992 Married Michelle Robinson

1995 His memoir, *Dreams from My Father,*
was published

1996 Elected as an Illinois state senator

1999 Daughter Malia was born

2000 Re-elected as an Illinois state senator

2001 Daughter Natasha (Sasha) was born

2004 Elected as a United States senator from Illinois

2006 His book, *The Audacity of Hope: Thoughts on Reclaiming the American Dream,* was published

2007 Declared as a candidate for president

2008 Selected as the Democratic candidate for president on August 27; the first African-American to be nominated by a major party

2008 Elected as the first African-American president of the United States

Glossary

civil rights	the rights of freedom for all citizens
campaign	the competition between political candidates
candidacy	running for election
convention	a meeting of a political party to nominate candidates
doctorate	the degree or title of doctor
election	the selection of a person for office decided by vote
liberal	beliefs that are more open-minded and willing to include all sides
nominate	to select someone to run for office

open-minded   willing to listen to other
                     opinions

political science the study of how government
                     works

prejudice   being against or biased
                     toward people for unfair
                     reasons

racism   treating people unfairly
                     because of their race

scholarship   money given to a student to
                     pay for school

senator   a member of the U.S. Senate,
                     the upper house in the U.S.
                     Government that makes laws

Learn More

Books

The Audacity of Hope: Thoughts on Reclaiming the American Dream by Barack Obama (Crown, 2006)

Barack Obama, An American Story by Roberta Edwards (Grosset and Dunlap, 2008)

Barack Obama: In His Own Words edited by Lisa Rogak (Carroll and Graf, 2007)

Barack Obama: Son of Promise, Child of Hope by Nikki Grimes (Simon and Schuster, 2008)

Dreams from My Father: A Story of Race and Inheritance by Barack Obama (Crown, 2004)

Yes We Can, A Biography of Barack Obama by Garen Thomas (Feiwel and Friends, 2008)

Video

Barack Obama's Speeches:
www.barackobama.com/tv/

Websites

www.barackobama.com
www.biography.com

Index